SCIENCE WORLD

STRUCTURES
AND MATERIALS

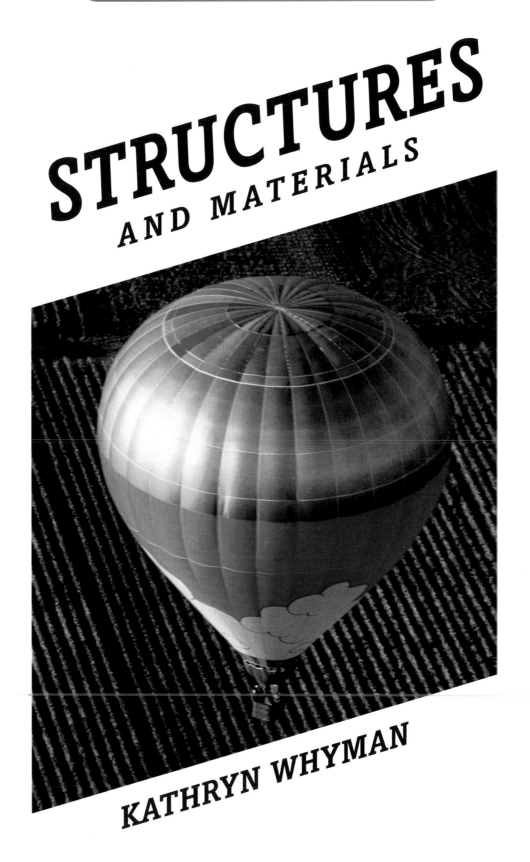

KATHRYN WHYMAN

Stargazer Books

© Aladdin Books Ltd 2005

New edition published in the United States in 2005 by:
Stargazer Books
c/o The Creative Company
123 South Broad Street
P.O. Box 227
Mankato, Minnesota 56002

Printed in UAE

Editor: Katie Harker

Designer: Flick, Book Design
& Graphics, Simon Morse

Illustrator: Louise Nevett

Picture Researcher:
Brian Hunter Smart

Library of Congress Cataloging-in-Publication Data

Whyman, Kathryn.
  Structures and materials / Kathryn Whyman.
    p. cm.
  Includes index.
  ISBN 1-932799-26-5
  1. Materials--Juvenile literature.
  2. Structural engineering--Juvenile literature. I. Title

TA403.2.W49 2004
620.1'1—dc22   2003070758

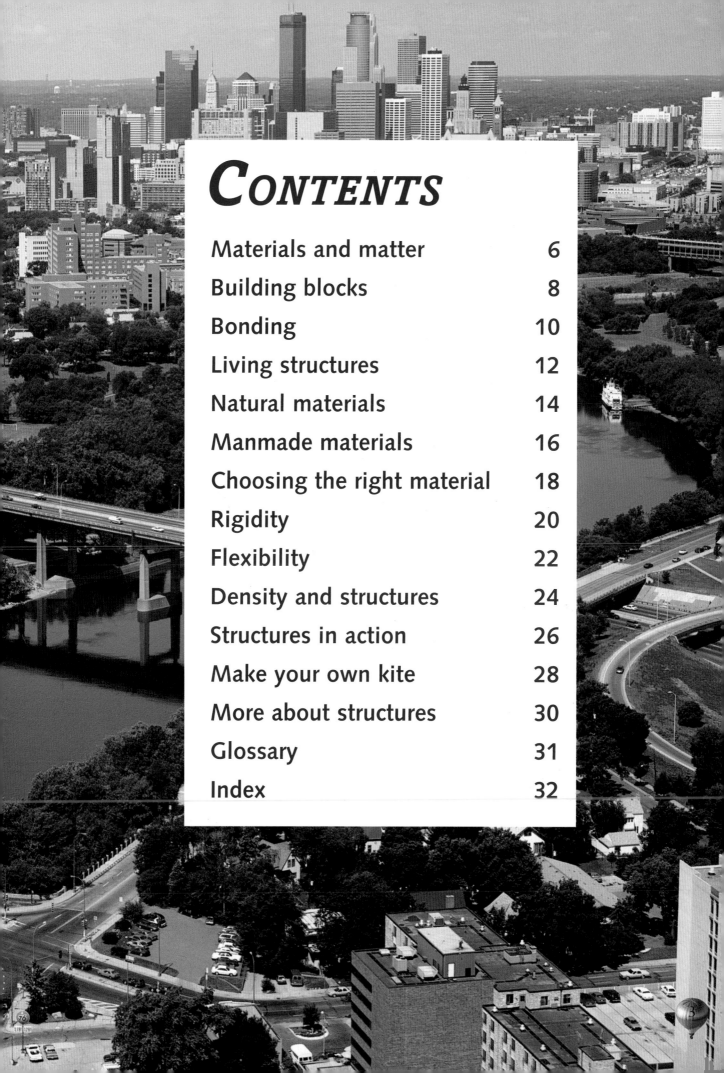

CONTENTS

INTRODUCTION

Look at the things around you and you will notice that all objects have a certain structure—they are put together in a particular way. We recognize many everyday objects, such as flowers, furniture, buildings, or parts of our bodies, by their familiar structures.

All structures are made up of materials. There are thousands of different materials in the world, both natural and manmade. The design of a structure and the materials used must be suitable for the particular purpose of that structure.

 Walls made entirely of stone—one of the oldest and most durable building materials

In this book you will learn more about structures and materials. You will begin to understand why things have a particular structure, and how design can affect the way that a structure works.

You will also find out why structures are made from certain materials—from the natural resources of the world around us, to artificial resources made by man. Knowing about different structures will help you to recognize the design and purpose of many everyday objects.

The Eiffel Tower, Paris, France. Made from iron, this giant structure is over 1,000ft high.

A giraffe's long neck helps it reach the leaves in the treetops.

MATERIALS AND MATTER

Materials are the substances from which things are made—like water, wood, iron, and plastics. All materials are made up of "matter." Matter is a more scientific word for the "stuff" that things are made from.

Materials can be put into one or more of three groups: solids, liquids, and gases. These are the three "states of matter." Materials may change from one state to another when they are heated or cooled. When a volcano erupts, red hot liquid is forced through the earth's surface where it quickly cools and becomes solid rock.

This is how the earth looks from outer space. You can see areas of land (which are solid) and sea (which are liquid). Surrounding the earth is the atmosphere (a mixture of gases).

Active volcanoes occasionally erupt boiling liquid rock (lava) from deep within the earth.

BUILDING BLOCKS

All materials are made up of "atoms." Atoms are tiny building blocks. Just as toy building blocks can be used to make a toy house, or bricks can be stacked to make a wall, atoms can join together to make up a material.

However, atoms are so small that they can only be seen using high-powered microscopes! Scientists have found that atoms join together in groups called "molecules." Each material has its own special type of molecules. These molecules give a material its unique characteristics.

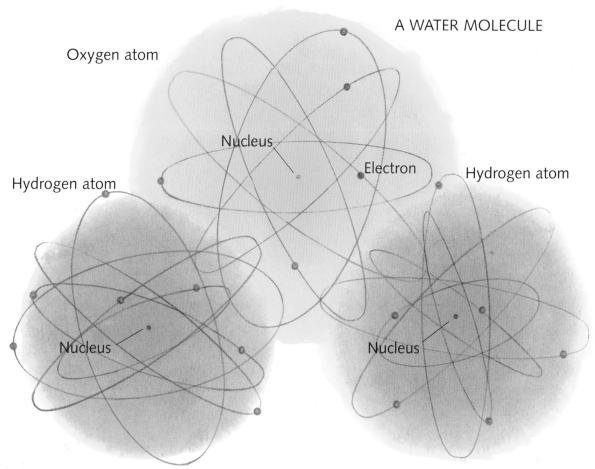

A WATER MOLECULE

Oxygen atom

Nucleus

Electron

Hydrogen atom

Hydrogen atom

Nucleus

Nucleus

Atoms and molecules

The diagram shows how a molecule of water might look. Water is made up of three atoms: two hydrogen and one oxygen. Both types of atom have a nucleus and tiny particles called electrons. Each hydrogen atom has one electron and each oxygen atom has eight electrons. The lines in the diagram show the electrons moving around the nucleus.

The molecules that make up glass are different from the molecules that make up water or paper. Yet, all atoms have the same basic structure: a nucleus surrounded by electrons.

Atoms join together to form a material, just as toy building blocks join to make a structure.

BONDING

The molecules in a solid material hold each other very tightly together. We say that "bonds" exist between the molecules that keep them in place. Molecules of solids are usually arranged into definite shapes called "crystals."

The bonds in some solids are stronger than in others. You could crush a salt crystal easily, but you would need special tools to split a diamond crystal. Solids have stronger bonds than liquids. That is why it is harder to put your hand through ice than water. The molecules in a gas do not have bonds between them. The bonds are broken when a liquid "evaporates" into a gas. Some materials are made of molecules that form strong bonds with molecules of other materials. We call these "adhesives," or glues.

Paper is a solid material. It is easy enough to tear most types of paper with your hands. But you will find it impossible to pull a whole sheet of paper apart. The bonds between the molecules of paper are very strong and cannot be separated unless you use all your strength on one small area.

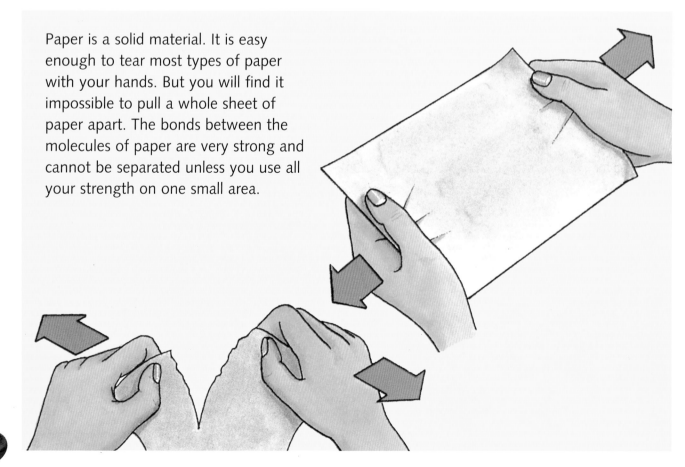

When water freezes, its molecules spread farther apart to form crystals of ice or snow.

Carbon fiber, used to make this boat, is tough because its molecules have strong bonds.

LIVING STRUCTURES

Living things are made of "cells"—tiny structures that you can only see with the aid of a microscope, though each cell contains millions of molecules! Human and animal cells are soft—they do not provide support or give a definitive shape. Instead, humans and most animals have a skeleton of bones to support the body, protect delicate organs, and help the body to move.

Plants do not need a skeleton of bones. Each of their cells is surrounded by a "wall" of material called "cellulose." As long as the cells have enough water they can support the plant. Some special cells form "veins" through the plant, which help to transport water and nutrients.

The diagram shows a section through a vein in a leaf. You can see that the leaf is made up of different types of cells. Cells on the leaf surface are wax-coated to stop the leaf from drying out. The cells that make up the veins carry food and water around the plant, and provide support.

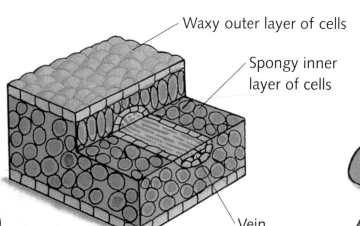

Waxy outer layer of cells

Spongy inner layer of cells

Vein

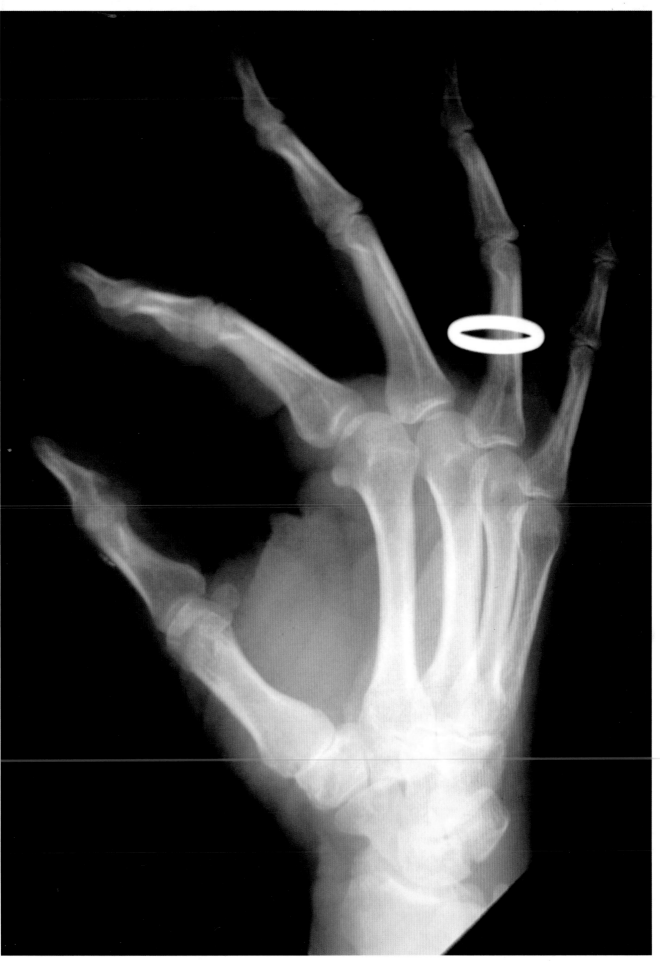

This X-ray shows the many bones of the hand that enable us to perform delicate tasks.

*N*ATURAL MATERIALS

For centuries, materials that occur naturally in the world around us have been used to build everyday structures. Over the years, wood and stone proved to be reliable construction materials and gradually these materials have been used together to make more complex structures.

Some natural materials need to be purified (refined), separated, or extracted before we can use them. Oil is refined to give a range of materials, from wax to gasoline. Metals are separated from their ores and salt is separated from seawater or rock salt. Combining and treating natural materials can also produce artificial or "manmade" materials.

This stone pyramid was built around 2600 BC as a burial chamber for Egyptian kings.

Oil is extracted from deep underground.

Copper ore: the basis of many metal products.

Making glass

Glass is made mostly of sand—small, loose grains that come from rocks weathered by the action of winds, rivers, waves, or glaciers. The world's largest deposits of sand are found in the deserts and on beaches. Glass is made by mixing sand with soda ash and limestone. When these substances are heated in a furnace at high temperatures they melt and join together to make glass. Sand is also used extensively in the manufacture of bricks, mortar, cement, concrete, plaster, and paving materials.

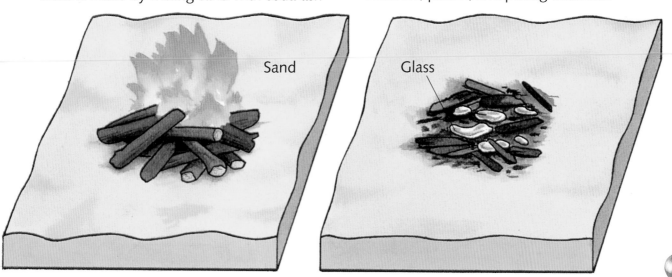

Sand

Glass

MANMADE MATERIALS

Today, many of our major industries are involved in the production of manmade materials. Look around and you will see numerous structures made from these. Steel, plastic, and glass are all manmade materials that are manufactured from natural resources. Steel is made from iron, plastic is made from chemicals found in oil, and glass is mostly made from sand.

Manmade materials have been developed over the years because they have special properties suited for a particular job. Advances in technology have meant that today, in some cases, manmade materials are also easier and cheaper to manufacture.

Glass is perfect for making windows. It can also be molded into shapes or thin fibers.

Plastics

Plastics are usually made from chemicals that come from oil. Plastics are cheap, easy to make, light, and they do not rust or rot. For these reasons plastics are often used instead of metal, wood, or glass. The properties of plastics vary according to their chemical structure. Some plastic structures, like these bags (right), are flexible. Others are rigid, transparent, or strong.

These steel cables are strong and flexible. Steel can also be toughened by adding carbon.

CHOOSING THE RIGHT MATERIAL

Not only must a structure have the right shape, it must also be made of a suitable material. Which material you choose will depend on its properties and the job that the structure is going to be used for.

It is sensible to make the windows of a house out of glass because it is transparent, and the walls out of bricks because they are strong. The cost of the material is also an important factor to think about. You may think that silk would be the best material to make dusters, but it would be quite a waste of money!

- Aluminum
- Steel
- Carbon fiber / reinforced plastic
- Fire-resistant materials
- Plastics
- Paint

Various materials have been chosen to make this aircraft. The framework is strong, the wings and body are light, the interior is colorful, and the fittings are fire resistant and easily molded.

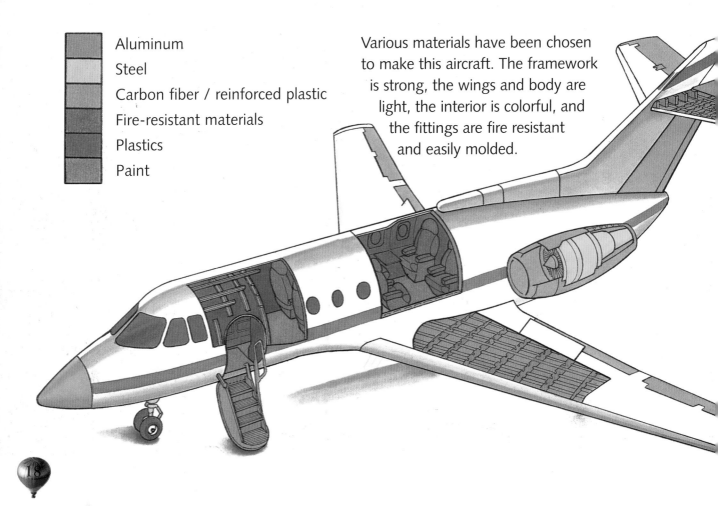

Different bicycle designs suit different purposes. A racing bike has slick tires on narrow wheels while an off-road bike has fat tires and a sturdy frame. Steel frames are cheap and relatively rust-resistant. Aluminum is a lighter alternative. Titanium is slightly flexible so it gives a smoother ride.

Carbon fiber is used to make boat masts because it can withstand large forces and is flexible.

RIGIDITY

You may have noticed that some animals, like giraffes or young foals, splay their legs as they try to stand upright. By making a triangle with their legs and the surface of the ground, they make themselves more stable. Tents are often designed with triangular frameworks for the same reason. This structure is less likely to collapse in windy weather. Triangular shapes are "rigid"—they cannot change.

A strong structure also needs the right materials. The molecules of some solids are arranged in rigid patterns. These materials can only bend very slightly and are likely to break—they are "brittle." For this reason, a standard glass rod will break more easily than one made of steel.

Keeping stable

Three sticks can be joined together to form a triangle. The joints are pivoted, but it is impossible to change the shape of the triangle unless you break it—it is rigid.

But if sticks are used to make a square, and you push the corners of the square to change its shape, or even flatten it, you can see that this shape is not rigid.

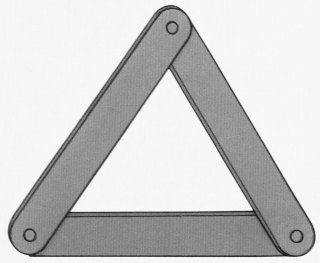

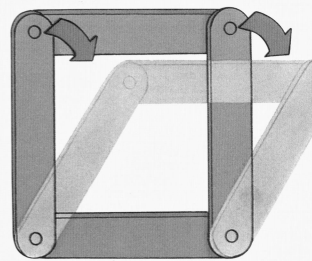

The triangular structure of the Eiffel Tower in Paris, France, keeps it strong and rigid.

FLEXIBILITY

Materials that bend or change shape when they are pushed or pulled are "flexible." Some materials, like rubber, are flexible because they are "elastic." You can stretch a rubber band, but it will return to its original shape when you let it go. Other materials, like metals, can return to their original shape even when a very large force is applied. These materials are useful for building strong structures.

Tall buildings are designed to be flexible and will sway a little in the wind. Trees are also flexible, although strong winds may sometimes stretch them too far! Even our bones are flexible while we are young. As we get older, they become more brittle and likely to break.

Diving boards are made from wood, fiberglass, or aluminum. Fiberglass and aluminum make the most flexible boards, enabling a diver to jump high over the water before entry.

This rubber ball is a sphere. When it drops to the ground, the ground exerts a force on it and the ball changes shape. But as the ball bounces upward and the force from the ground is removed, it once again becomes spherical. The rubber ball is elastic.

The flexible trunks of palm trees allow them to bend in the wind.

25

DENSITY AND STRUCTURES

If you hold a block of cork in one hand and a block of glass of exactly the same shape and size in the other, you will notice that the glass feels heavier than the cork. We say that glass is more "dense" than cork.

But what makes some materials more dense than others? It may be that the molecules are heavier, or they may be packed more closely together. Solids are often more dense than liquids for this reason. Yet, many solids are less dense than liquids. Ice, for example, floats on water because its molecules are farther apart.

Birds are able to remain in the air easily as they fly. Their wings are specially designed for this purpose. One feature of the wings is that their bones contain large air spaces. Because these bones consist of the bone tissue and air, they are less dense than they would be if they were solid bone. This structure also makes the bones stronger and less likely to break.

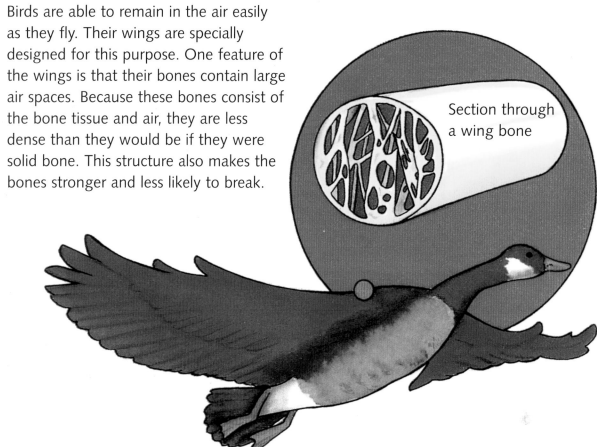

Section through a wing bone

24

Hot air is less dense than cool air, causing these hot air balloons to float upward.

STRUCTURES IN ACTION

All structures are designed to do particular jobs. Every structure of your body has its own shape—from the hard, sharp teeth you use for biting, to the strong, flexible feet on which you walk. Every object in the room around you, however simple, also has a shape suitable for its purpose.

Some of the structures we build are very complicated. A bridge must support its own weight and the weight of the vehicles traveling across it. Suspension bridges literally hang from thick cables stretched over massive supports. Strong, taut wires join the bridge to the cables.

Light but strong

Aircraft wings are not made of solid metal —this would be too heavy. But they have to be strong. The insides of the wings are often made up of a framework of six-sided aluminum "cells" filled with air.

Honeybees have been using this sort of structure since long before aircraft were invented! Their honeycombs, which house their young and store their food, are strong and make good use of space.

Aluminum honeycomb structure used for aircraft

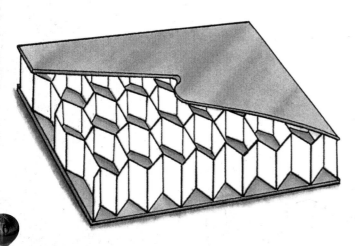

Bee honeycomb

Muscle

Tendon

Joint

Our skeleton is not a totally rigid structure—it has joints that allow us to move. This diagram shows the structure of an elbow joint. The joint is rather like the hinge on a door. Muscles, attached to the bones by strong tendons, contract (shorten) or relax (lengthen) to move the bones of the arm up or down.

The Golden Gate suspension bridge, San Francisco

MAKE YOUR OWN KITE

This kite is a simple structure that you can build from everyday materials—and it is fun to fly, too! Your kite must be made from light, yet strong and flexible materials. Plastic is used to cover the frame which is made from light wood. It makes a light, strong structure.

A kite's special structure means that it can soar in the wind.

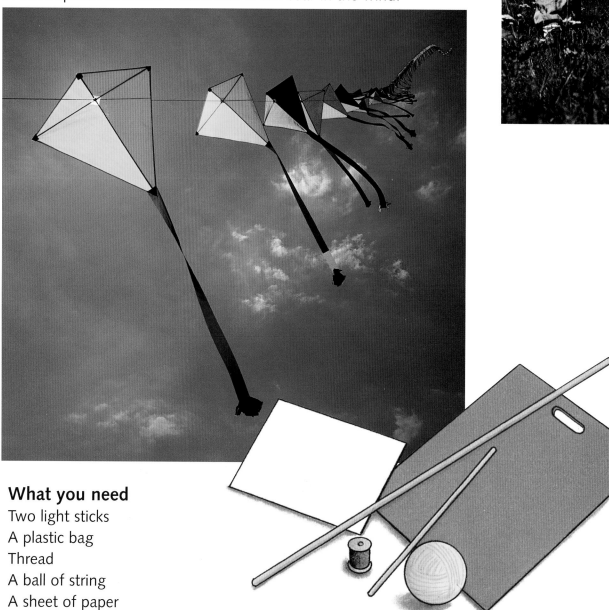

What you need
Two light sticks
A plastic bag
Thread
A ball of string
A sheet of paper

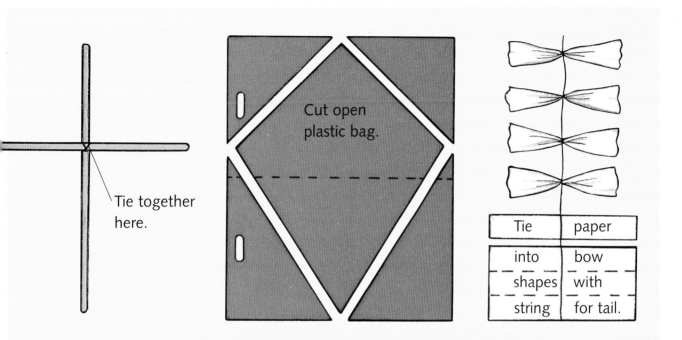

Tie together here.

Cut open plastic bag.

Tie	paper
into	bow
shapes	with
string	for tail.

Make a framework by tying two sticks firmly together. This framework gives you the shape for your kite. Now cut open the plastic bag and cut a piece to fit your framework. You can make your kite more balanced by giving it a tail of plastic (see photo, far left) or string and folded paper (see below left). Join all the parts of the kite together. The corners must be tied securely, first with thread and then with string. Make sure the ball of string is attached to all four corners.

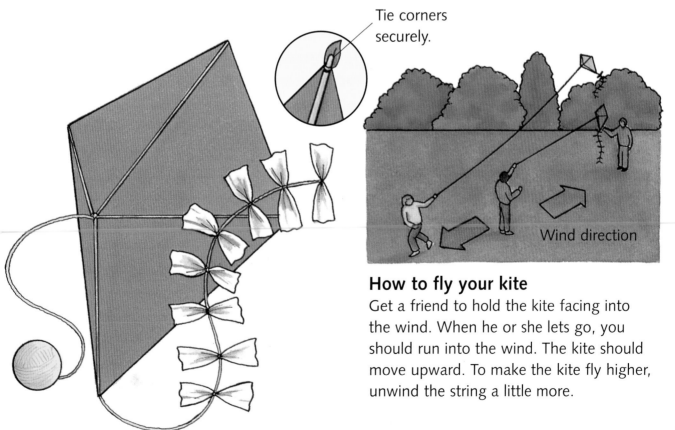

Tie corners securely.

Wind direction

How to fly your kite

Get a friend to hold the kite facing into the wind. When he or she lets go, you should run into the wind. The kite should move upward. To make the kite fly higher, unwind the string a little more.

MORE ABOUT STRUCTURES

The structure of an atom

All atoms have the same basic structure. The central nucleus is the heaviest part of the atom. It is made up of two types of particle: neutrons and protons. Neutrons have no "charge," but the protons each carry a positive charge. So the nucleus is shown with a plus sign.

Traveling around the nucleus are particles we call electrons. These particles have a negative charge, so we show them with a minus sign. Since the atom has the same number of positive and negative charges, they balance each other out. The atom is "neutral."

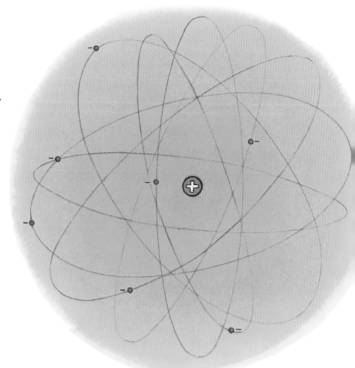

Bonding structures

Salt is made up of atoms of sodium and chlorine. When a pair of these atoms comes together, it behaves in a special way. One of the electrons belonging to the sodium atom moves toward the chlorine atom. Now the charges of the atoms are no longer balanced. The sodium atom has an extra positive charge and the chlorine has an extra negative charge. We call the sodium a positive "ion" and the chlorine a negative ion. In salt, the sodium and chlorine ions are bonded together by a balance of these charges. This balance gives the salt molecule its cubic shape.

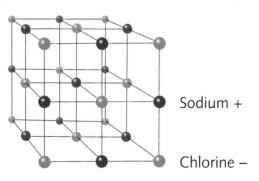

Sodium +

Chlorine –

GLOSSARY

Adhesive
A substance used for sticking objects together. Also called glue. Adhesives are often made from animal bones, hoofs, and tree resins.

Atom
A tiny particle. It is the smallest part of an element that can exist and still have all the characteristics of that element.

Bond
The force that holds atoms together to form molecules.

Carbon fiber
A black silky thread of pure carbon made by heating and stretching textile fibers. Because of its lightness and strength at high temperatures, carbon fiber is used to reinforce plastic, metal, and glass.

Cell
A very small part of living matter. Different kinds of cells do different jobs in the body of a plant or animal.

Cellulose
A natural substance made up of long chains of molecules. It forms the walls of plant cells.

Crystals
Formed when a pure substance becomes a solid. Crystals have a definite shape with edges, corners, and flat surfaces.

Density
Mass compared to volume. Solids are often denser than liquids.

Electron
A tiny particle of matter in orbit around the nucleus of an atom. It has a negative electric charge.

Evaporate
To change a liquid into a gas, often by heating.

Hydrogen
A very light gas. Hydrogen atoms are also found in compounds such as water.

Materials
Substances from which something is made.

Molecule
Two or more atoms that exist as a group. A molecule is the smallest part of a compound that can exist on its own and still have all the characteristics of that compound.

Neutron
One of the tiny particles in the nucleus of all atoms (except hydrogen). Neutrons have no electric charge.

Nucleus
The center of an atom, which contains tiny particles called protons and neutrons.

Ore
Any naturally occurring mineral from which metal can be extracted.

Oxygen
A colorless gas that makes up about a fifth of the air we breathe. Oxygen atoms are also found in a variety of other substances including water.

Properties
Characteristics that describe the appearance or behavior of a substance in different conditions.

Proton
A tiny particle in the nucleus of all atoms. Protons have a positive charge.

Refined
Separated into various pure substances.

INDEX

Photocredits Abbreviations: l-left, r-right, b-bottom, t-top, c-center, m-middle. Front cover main, back cover main, 2-3, 4tl, 4tr, 6tl, 8tl, 10tl, 11t, 12tl, 14tl, 14tr, 16tl, 18tl, 19 both, 20 both, 22tl, 22c, 24tl, 26tl, 27, 28tl, 30t, 31t, 32t — Photodisc. Front cover mt, 10tr, 30br — NASA. Front cover mb, 1, 5b, 6tr, 7, 16tr, 21, 26tr — Digital Stock. 4b, 16b, 17 inset — Corel. 5tr — Photo Essentials. 6br, 9 main, 13, 14b, 18tr, 23, 24tr, 28tr — Corbis. 8tr — Brian Hunter Smart. 9 inset — PBD. 11b — Scania. 12tr — USDA. 15tl — Comstock. 15tr — National Park Service. 17 main — Flat Earth. 22tr — Ingram Publishing. 25 — Tony Stone Associates. 28ml — Corbis Royalty Free.